WORLD OF INSECTS

Wasps

by Martha E. H. Rustad

BLASTOFF! READERS
2

BELLWETHER MEDIA · MINNEAPOLIS, MN

Note to Librarians, Teachers, and Parents:

Blastoff! Readers are carefully developed by literacy experts and combine standards-based content with developmentally-appropriate text.

Level 1 provides the most support through repetition of high-frequency words, light text, predictable sentence patterns, and strong visual support.

Level 2 offers early readers a bit more challenge through varied simple sentences, increased text load, and less repetition of high frequency words.

Level 3 advances early-fluent readers toward fluency through increased text and concept load, less reliance on visuals, longer sentences, and more literary language.

Level 4 builds reading stamina by providing more text per page, increased use of punctuation, greater variation in sentence patterns, and increasingly challenging vocabulary.

Level 5 encourages children to move from "learning to read" to "reading to learn" by providing even more text, varied writing styles, and less familiar topics.

Whichever book is right for your reader, Blastoff! Readers are the perfect books to build confidence and encourage a love of reading that will last a lifetime!

This edition first published in 2008 by Bellwether Media.

No part of this publication may be reproduced in whole or in part without written permission of the publisher. For information regarding permission, write to Bellwether Media Inc., Attention: Permissions Department, Post Office Box 1C, Minnetonka, MN 55345-9998.

Library of Congress Cataloging-in-Publication Data
Rustad, Martha E. H. (Martha Elizabeth Hillman), 1975–
    Wasps / by Martha E.H. Rustad.
      p. cm. – (Blastoff! readers. World of insects)
Summary: "Simple text accompanied by full-color photographs give an upclose look at wasps. Intended for kindergarten through third grade students"—Provided by publisher.
    Includes bibliographical references and index.
    ISBN-13: 978-1-60014-076-1 (hardcover : alk. paper)
    ISBN-10: 1-60014-076-9 (hardcover : alk. paper)
    1. Wasps—Juvenile literature. I. Title.

QL565.2.R87 2008
595.79–dc22   2007009770

Contents

front wing

rear wing

Wasps are **insects** with four
narrow wings.

They move their wings quickly to fly. Moving wings make a buzzing sound.

waist

There are many kinds of wasps. Most have a skinny **waist**.

Some have colorful bodies.

Many wasps drink **nectar** from flowers.

They sip nectar through
their mouths.

Many wasps also eat other insects. They eat them with their strong jaws.

Wasps eat **pests**. Pests kill **crops**. Wasps help crops stay healthy.

Many female wasps have
a **stinger**. They sting other
insects to kill them for food.

Some wasps may also sting animals or people who bother them. Their stings are painful.

Many wasps build **nests** for their young. Wasps build different kinds of nests.

Some wasps dig a hole in
the ground for a nest.

Some wasps build a mud
cave for a nest.

Other wasps make
paper nests.

These wasps chew plants and wood and spit them out as a paste.

They build their nest with the paste. It dries and looks like paper.

Hundreds of wasps can live in one paper nest.

Wasps will sting to **defend** their nest. Always be careful around wasp nests.

Glossary

crops—plants people grow for food

defend—to protect from danger; wasps will sting to defend their nest.

insect—a kind of animal with six legs; most insects also have a hard body, two antennas, and two or four wings.

nectar—sweet juice made by flowers

nest—a kind of home some animals build

pest—an animal or plant that damages something used by humans

stinger—a sharp body part on some insects and animals used for defense or to kill another animal for food; a wasp has poison in its stinger.

waist—a thin part in the middle of a wasp's body

To Learn More

AT THE LIBRARY

Frost, Helen. *Wasps. Insects.* Mankato, Minn.: Capstone Press, 2001.

Hall, Margaret. *Wasps.* Mankato, Minn.: Capstone Press, 2006.

Hirschmann, Kris. *Wasp. Bugs.* San Diego, Calif.: KidHaven Press, 2006.

Pyers, Greg. *Wasps Up Close.* Chicago, Ill.: Raintree, 2005.

ON THE WEB

Learning more about wasps is as easy as 1, 2, 3.

1. Go to www.factsurfer.com

2. Enter "wasps" into search box.

3. Click the "Surf" button and you will see a list of related web sites.

With factsurfer.com, finding more information is just a click away.

Index

The photographs in this book are reproduced through the courtesy of: Florin C, front cover; E.A. Janes, p. 4; Bob Jensen/Alamy, p. 5; Remigius Budhi Isworo, p. 6; Bartomeu Borrell, p. 7; Juniors Bildarchiv/Alamy, p. 8; Yaroslav, p. 9; Lukas Hejtman, pp. 10-11; Lasse Patterson/Getty Images, p. 13; TSWong, p. 14; WildPictures/Alamy, pp. 15, 16; Lorraine Swanson, p. 17; Grady Harrison/Alamy, pp. 18-19; Stephen St. John/Getty Images, pp. 20-21.